How to Say the Obvious Without Being Rude: The Art of Clear and Objective Communication

Copyright © 2024 Reginaldo Osnildo
All rights reserved.

PRESENTATION..4
INTRODUCTION TO EFFECTIVE COMMUNICATION.........7
THE PERCEPTION OF THE OBVIOUS 11
PRINCIPLES OF NON-AGGRESSIVE COMMUNICATION..15
THE IMPORTANCE OF EMPATHY 19
CHOOSING THE RIGHT MOMENT 23
BODY LANGUAGE AND NONVERBAL COMMUNICATION
....27
ACTIVE LISTENING 31
POSITIVE FRAMING 35
AVOIDING COMMUNICATION PITFALLS.......................39
THE ART OF ASKING 43
ASSERTIVENESS VS. AGGRESSIVENESS 47
CONSTRUCTIVE FEEDBACK..51
TRAINING PATIENCE AND CONTROL 55
MINDFULNESS TECHNIQUES IN COMMUNICATION 59
PRACTICAL CASES: HOW TO SAY THE OBVIOUS
WITHOUT BEING ROUGH 63
BUILDING BRIDGES, NOT WALLS...................................67
RESOLVING CONFLICTS WITH ELEGANCE.....................71
CULTIVATING HUMILITY IN COMMUNICATION 75
DEVELOPING GENTLE PERSUASION SKILLS 79

DIGITAL COMMUNICATION AND ETIQUETTE 83
OVERCOMING CULTURAL BARRIERS 88
SELF-CARE AND SELF-AWARENESS 92
CREATING AN OPENING ENVIRONMENT 97
RECEIVE AND INTEGRATE FEEDBACK 101
CONCLUSION AND THE WAY FORWARD 105
REGINALDO OSNILDO 110

PRESENTATION

Welcome to the beginning of a transformative journey with the book **"How to Say the Obvious Without Being Rude: The Art of Clear and Objective Communication"**. If you've ever found yourself in a situation where expressing a simple idea seems more complicated than it should be, or if you have a desire to improve your communication skills to strengthen your relationships both personally and professionally, you're in the right place. .

This book is an invitation to explore the art of communicating thoughts and facts that may seem obvious, but require sensitivity and clarity to be shared without misunderstanding or offense. Through the following pages, you will discover methods and techniques that will not only illuminate the way you express yourself, but also completely transform your interactions with others.

"How to Say the Obvious Without Being Rude: The Art of Clear and Objective Communication" is more than a manual; It is a companion in your personal development. Here, I bring an updated perspective on classic communication concepts, adapting them to contemporary needs to facilitate their application in everyday life. Each chapter in this book has been carefully crafted to complete, offering you a gradual and in-depth learning experience.

Get ready to dive into a practical approach that will equip you with the tools you need to face communication challenges with confidence and grace. By mastering the strategies presented, you will not only understand how to speak effectively, but also how to do so in a way that builds bridges, not walls.

Yours sincerely

Reginaldo Osnildo

INTRODUCTION TO EFFECTIVE COMMUNICATION

Communicating effectively is a fundamental skill in all areas of life: at work, in personal relationships and even in our internal dialogue. Mastering this art is essential for anyone who wants to be understood and understand others without misunderstandings or conflicts. In this chapter, you will explore the importance of expressing your ideas and opinions clearly and respectfully, laying a strong foundation for the more specific concepts we will cover in the following chapters.

THE VALUE OF CLEAR COMMUNICATION

Clarity in communication goes beyond the correct use of words; it's about conveying your message in such a way that it is effortlessly understood by the interlocutor. This involves both the choice of words and the timing, tone and context in which they are said. Effective communication can prevent a large number of misunderstandings and mistakes that occur simply because the parties involved fail to understand each other.

ELEMENTS OF EFFECTIVE COMMUNICATION

- **Clarity and conciseness:** Be direct and to the point, avoiding using jargon or an excess of words that can confuse the listener.

- **Appropriate tone:** Adjust your tone of voice to match the situation, which could mean being more formal in a work environment or more relaxed at home.

- **Active feedback:** Engage the listener by requesting feedback to confirm that the message was received and understood as intended.

- **Empathy:** Showing consideration and understanding for the other's emotions and situation, which can completely transform the reception of your message.

- **Active listening:** Show your interlocutor that you value their words by actively listening and responding in a way that demonstrates that you understood what was said.

Throughout this book, you will see how these elements are applied in different situations to ensure that even points that may seem obvious are communicated effectively and kindly.

WHY IS IT SO DIFFICULT TO SAY THE OBVIOUS?

Often, what seems obvious to you may not be so clear to someone else, due to differences in background, experiences or even emotional state. Therefore, assuming that everyone shares your point of view can lead to misunderstandings and defensive responses. In this book, you will learn to identify when and how to express the obvious, ensuring that your message is not only heard, but accepted and understood.

This chapter is just the beginning. Are you ready to advance your journey towards effective communication? In the next chapter, **"THE PERCEPTION OF THE OBVIOUS"**, we will explore how different experiences and perspectives influence what each of us considers obvious. Let's discover how to adjust our communication so that it resonates with any audience, expanding our ability to be effective and respectful communicators. I'll see you there!

THE PERCEPTION OF THE OBVIOUS

In this chapter, we will explore a crucial concept in communication: the perception of the obvious. What is considered evident to one person may not be so clear to another, influenced by a myriad of factors such as culture, life experience, prior knowledge and emotional context. Understanding this diversity of perceptions is essential for you to improve your ability to communicate your ideas clearly and without causing offense.

UNDERSTANDING THE RELATIVITY OF THE OBVIOUS

The obvious is, in many cases, a subjective concept. For example, something that is routine and self-evident in a professional technology environment may be completely foreign and complex to someone outside of that industry. This difference in understanding can create significant communicative barriers if not recognized and managed carefully.

FACTORS THAT INFLUENCE THE PERCEPTION OF THE OBVIOUS

> **- Personal experience:** The accumulation of personal experiences shapes what we consider obvious. For example, a person who grew up in a big city may find it obvious how to navigate a complex public transportation system, while someone from a rural area may find this task challenging.

- **Cultural context:** Cultural differences can profoundly influence what is perceived as evident. Gestures, facial expressions, and even the use of certain words can have varying meanings in different cultures.

- **Education and knowledge:** A person's level of education and area of knowledge also define much of what they perceive as obvious. Professionals in different fields have jargon and knowledge bases that may be obscure to the general public.

- **Emotional state:** The emotional state at the time of communication can affect how messages are interpreted. Stress, anxiety or even excessive joy can distort the perception of what is said.

HOW TO NAVIGATE DIFFERENCES IN PERCEPTION OF THE OBVIOUS

- **Always clarify:** Never assume that your message is universally understood. Clarify points that may be seen as obvious to you but may not be obvious to others.

- **Adapt your message:** Know your audience and adapt your message according to their level of understanding and experience. This may involve simplifying language, using analogies, or providing more context.

- **Ask for feedback:** Encourage questions and feedback to ensure your message is understood. This also shows respect and appreciation for the other person's perspective.

- **Be patient:** Recognize that explaining something that is obvious to you may require patience. Maintain an attitude of openness and support, rather than frustration or condescension.

This chapter revealed how the obvious can be surprisingly complex. Ready to continue deepening your knowledge of effective communication? In the next chapter, **"PRINCIPLES OF NON-AGGRESSIVE COMMUNICATION"**, we will explore how you can express the obvious in a constructive and empathetic way, avoiding being perceived as rude or insensitive. Join us to discover strategies to keep your interactions as clear as they are friendly. Let's go?

PRINCIPLES OF NON-AGGRESSIVE COMMUNICATION

When developing the ability to communicate the obvious without being rude, one of the most important aspects is non-aggressive communication. This chapter explores the fundamentals of how to express your ideas and thoughts in a constructive and empathetic way, ensuring that you preserve healthy relationships and foster an environment of mutual understanding.

WHAT IS NON-AGGRESSIVE COMMUNICATION?

Non-aggressive communication is an approach that focuses on clarity, empathy and respect in interactions. It aims to express your needs and feelings without causing defense or aggression in the other person. This method is especially useful when you need to address sensitive topics or when you are dealing with conversations that involve strong emotions.

PILLARS OF NON-AGGRESSIVE COMMUNICATION

>   **- Observe without evaluating:** Start by observing what happens without attributing judgments or personal interpretations. This helps maintain objectivity and clarity in communication.

>   **- Express feelings:** Communicate your feelings clearly. Use statements that begin with "I feel" to express your own emotions without implying that the other person is responsible for them.

- **Identify needs:** Clarify what your needs are or what you expect from the conversation. By expressing your needs clearly, you give the other person the opportunity to understand your point of view without ambiguity.

- **Make requests, not demands:** When expressing what you want, make clear requests that are open to negotiation, rather than demands. This allows the other person space to respond without feeling pressured or coerced.

APPLYING NON-AGGRESSIVE COMMUNICATION

- **Professional situations:** When dealing with co-workers or in negotiations, non-aggressive communication can help maintain a professional and respectful environment. For example, instead of saying "You never pay attention in meetings," try "I feel like my ideas aren't being considered during meetings. Could you help me understand how I can make myself more heard?"

- **Personal relationships:** In more intimate relationships, this approach can prevent conflicts and strengthen bonds. Expressing needs and feelings clearly and directly can avoid misunderstandings and resentment.

- **Self-communication:** Even in the way you talk to yourself, non-aggressive communication can be beneficial. Instead of harshly criticizing yourself, acknowledge your feelings and needs, treating yourself with compassion and understanding.

This chapter provides the foundation for you to state the obvious in a way that is beneficial and positive, always maintaining an attitude of respect and consideration for the feelings and perspectives of others. Ready to move forward? In the next chapter, **"THE IMPORTANCE OF EMPATHY"**, we will explore more deeply how putting yourself in someone else's shoes can transform the way you communicate. Together, we will learn how crucial this skill is for truly effective and kind communication. Shall we continue this journey of discovery?

THE IMPORTANCE OF EMPATHY

Empathy is the ability to understand and share another person's feelings. It is a fundamental element in communication, as it allows you to see situations from other perspectives and respond in a more appropriate and sensitive way. In this chapter, we will explore how to develop and apply empathy in your daily interactions to improve the clarity of communication and avoid misunderstandings or offense.

THE POWER OF EMPATHY IN COMMUNICATION

Empathizing with someone means more than simply understanding what the other person is feeling; it also involves an appropriate emotional response. This can be especially helpful when communicating ideas that seem obvious but may be sensitive or difficult for someone else to accept. Empathy helps smooth the delivery of messages that might otherwise be met with resistance or hostility.

HOW TO DEVELOP EMPATHY

- **Listen actively:** Dedicate yourself to really listening to what the other person is saying, without planning your response while they speak. This shows respect and genuine interest.

- **Put yourself in the other person's shoes:** Try to imagine yourself in the other person's situation, considering their life experiences and emotions. Ask yourself how you would feel in his position.

- **Observe non-verbal emotions:** Much of communication is non-verbal. Pay attention to body language, tone of voice, and facial expressions to pick up on what may not be being said directly.

- **Ask and clarify:** If you're not sure how the person is feeling, ask. This shows that you care about clarity of communication and are willing to fully understand her perspective.

APPLYING EMPATHY IN PRACTICE

- **Conflicts:** When conflicts arise, empathy can help understand the emotional roots of the problem. Communicating with empathy can defuse tensions and pave the way for constructive solutions.

- **Work environment:** At work, empathy helps create a more collaborative and less competitive environment. Understanding the pressures and challenges faced by colleagues can significantly improve team dynamics.

- **Personal relationships:** At home, practicing empathy can strengthen family and friendship bonds, allowing everyone to feel heard and valued.

By developing your ability to empathize, you not only improve your communication skills but also enrich your interpersonal relationships. Empathy is a powerful tool for ensuring your messages are delivered effectively and respectfully, promoting deeper and lasting understanding.

Ready to take your communication skills to a new level? In the next chapter, **"CHOOSING THE RIGHT MOMENT"**, we will explore strategies for identifying the most appropriate time to express your ideas, ensuring that your messages are received in the most favorable context possible. Follow us on this learning journey and discover how timing can be as crucial as the message itself.

CHOOSING THE RIGHT MOMENT

The effectiveness of communication depends not only on what is said, but also on when and how the words are expressed. Choosing the right time to bring up sensitive or glaring issues can make a significant difference in how your message is received. In this chapter, you will learn strategies for identifying the best time to communicate your ideas, increasing the chances of a constructive and responsive dialogue.

THE IMPORTANCE OF TIMING IN COMMUNICATION

Timing can amplify or diminish the impact of your words. A message delivered at the inappropriate time can generate misunderstandings, resistance or even conflicts, while the same message, if shared at the right time, can be received with openness and understanding.

FACTORS TO CONSIDER WHEN CHOOSING THE RIGHT TIME

- **Environmental context:** The environment in which the message is delivered can profoundly affect its reception. A quiet, private place is generally more conducive to serious discussions than a public or chaotic environment.

- **Emotional state:** Assessing the emotional state of the person receiving the message is crucial. Bringing up a sensitive topic when someone is already stressed or distracted can lead to a negative reaction.

- **Availability:** Make sure the person has time to really listen and engage in the conversation. A time when both of you are not in a rush or under pressure from other tasks is ideal.

- **Preparation:** Some conversations benefit from prior preparation. If necessary, let them know that you would like to discuss something important, giving the other person time to mentally prepare for the conversation.

STRATEGIES FOR CHOOSING THE APPROPRIATE MOMENT

- **Observe and learn:** Pay attention to the day-to-day patterns of the person you need to talk to. Identify moments when she is most relaxed and receptive.

- **Ask for permission:** Before starting a delicate conversation, ask if this is a good time. Not only does this ensure you get the attention you need, but it also shows respect for each other's time.

- **Be flexible:** Be willing to adjust your plans based on the other person's response. If it's not a good time, ask when it would be more convenient to resume the discussion.

By applying these strategies, you can significantly increase the effectiveness of your communication. Choosing the right moment shows consideration and respect for each other's needs and circumstances, establishing fertile ground for open and honest dialogue.

Ready to continue improving your communication skills? In the next chapter, **"BODY LANGUAGE AND NONVERBAL COMMUNICATION"** , we will explore how the nonverbal aspects of communication can help or hinder the delivery of your message. Join us to understand more about how your body speaks as much as your words.

BODY LANGUAGE AND NONVERBAL COMMUNICATION

Although words are powerful, much of communication happens through nonverbal means. Body language, eye contact, posture, and even tone of voice play crucial roles in how your messages are received and interpreted. In this chapter, we will explore the role of nonverbal communication in expressing messages clearly and non-aggressively, helping you understand how your gestures and expressions can reinforce or contradict your words.

THE INFLUENCE OF BODY LANGUAGE ON COMMUNICATION

Body language can convey confidence, openness, defensiveness or disinterest, among many other things. It is an essential tool for strengthening a verbal message, providing context that words alone may not be able to fully communicate.

KEY ELEMENTS OF NONVERBAL COMMUNICATION

- **Posture:** An open posture, with arms uncrossed and a slight inclination towards the interlocutor, can indicate interest and receptivity. On the other hand, a closed posture can be interpreted as defensive or disinterested.

- **Eye contact:** Maintaining balanced eye contact is crucial. Looking someone directly in the eye while speaking demonstrates confidence and sincerity. Avoiding eye contact, on the other hand, can be perceived as a lack of confidence or disinterest.

- **Facial expressions:** Your expressions must be in line with your message. A smile can soften a criticism, while a serious face can reinforce the importance of a warning or command.

- **Gestures:** Gestures can help emphasize important points or illustrate a concept. However, excessive or inappropriate gestures can distract or even confuse the interlocutor.

- **Proximity:** The physical distance between you and the person you are talking to also affects communication. Too close can be intimidating, while too far away can seem distant and disengaged.

HOW TO IMPROVE YOUR NONVERBAL COMMUNICATION

- **Body awareness:** Become more aware of your own body language. Practice being present and aware of what your body is doing as you speak.

- **Mirroring:** Try to subtly mirror the body language of whoever you are talking to. This can create a sense of empathy and mutual understanding.

- **Feedback:** Ask for feedback on how your nonverbal communication is perceived. This can be especially useful for adjusting behaviors you may not be aware of.

- **Adaptation:** Adapt your non-verbal communication according to the context and the person with whom you are interacting. What works in a casual setting may not be appropriate in a more formal context.

Understanding and effectively applying body language and other aspects of nonverbal communication can transform the way you interact with others, making your interactions more effective and harmonious.

Are you ready to continue deepening your communication skills? In the next chapter, **"ACTIVE LISTENING"** , we will explore how to develop your listening skills to better understand others' concerns and points of view before speaking. Follow us to discover strategies for listening more effectively and responsively. Let's go!

ACTIVE LISTENING

Active listening is one of the most important skills for effective communication. It not only allows you to truly understand what is being said, but also demonstrates respect and care for the interlocutor. In this chapter, we'll explore active listening techniques that will help you capture not just the words, but also the emotions and intentions behind them, significantly improving your personal and professional interactions.

WHAT IS ACTIVE LISTENING?

Active listening is an active process of listening carefully to what another is saying, involving both understanding the words and responding that shows you are engaged. It's more than just passive listening; It's about understanding, retaining, and responding appropriately to another's message.

FUNDAMENTAL ELEMENTS OF ACTIVE LISTENING

- **Full attention:** Focus completely on the speaker, avoiding distractions such as cell phones or wandering thoughts. This may involve direct eye contact and an open, receptive posture.

- **Do not interrupt:** Allow the speaker to finish their ideas without interruptions. This shows respect for your thoughts and feelings and avoids making hasty assumptions.

- **Reflect the content:** Paraphrase what the speaker said to confirm that you understood correctly. This also helps the speaker hear their own idea and potentially refine or expand their thinking.

- **Observe non-verbals:** Pay attention to body language, tone of voice and facial expressions to capture the complete message, including nuances that words alone cannot convey.

- **Respond empathetically:** Show empathy and validate the speaker's feelings, even if you don't agree with them. This can be done through comments that acknowledge their emotions or expressing understanding.

BENEFITS OF ACTIVE LISTENING

- **Improves relationships:** Builds trust and respect, fundamental for healthy and collaborative relationships.

- **Conflict prevention:** Reduces misunderstandings and promotes more effective conflict resolutions.

- **Greater understanding:** Increases the effectiveness of communication by enabling a deeper understanding of people's needs and concerns.

PUTTING IT INTO PRACTICE

- **Listening exercises:** Practice with friends or co-workers by asking them to share something and then you respond by summarizing what you understood.

- **Constant feedback:** Request feedback on how you are listening to continually improve your skills.

- **Diverse environments:** Use active listening in different contexts to understand how it can be adapted according to the needs of the situation and the people involved.

Mastering active listening is essential for anyone looking to improve their communication. Ready to move forward? In the next chapter, **"POSITIVE FRAMING"** , we will explore techniques for framing your message in a positive way, even when addressing sensitive or obvious topics. Be prepared to learn how your words can encourage a more open and cooperative reception. Let's go on this journey together!

POSITIVE FRAMING

The way you frame your communication can significantly influence how your message is received. "Positive framing" is a powerful technique that involves presenting information in a way that highlights the positive aspects, even when the topic under discussion may be sensitive or potentially negative. In this chapter, you will learn how to apply positive framing to transform challenging conversations into constructive and encouraging interactions.

WHAT IS POSITIVE FRAMING?

Positive framing refers to the practice of restructuring the way you present an idea or problem, focusing on the positive aspects or solutions rather than the difficulties or negative aspects. This approach not only improves acceptance of the message, but can also change the listener's perception and attitude towards the content discussed.

HOW TO USE POSITIVE FRAMING

- **Focus on solutions, not problems:** Instead of highlighting what is wrong or what is missing, focus on how things can be improved and what are the possible steps to achieve that improvement.

- **Use encouraging language:** Words have power. Choose terms that are positive and encouraging. For example, instead of saying "This isn't good," you could say "Let's see how we can make this better together."

- **Highlight the benefits:** When discussing changes or feedback, emphasize the benefits that will accompany the suggested changes. This can help create a more optimistic outlook and a greater willingness to accept.

- **Avoid negative language:** Words like "no", "never" and "nothing" can instigate resistance. Try to rephrase these expressions in a way that avoids negativity.

- **Be empathetic:** Acknowledge the concerns and feelings of others when presenting your message. This shows that you understand and respect their perspectives, which can facilitate a more positive reception.

BENEFITS OF POSITIVE FRAMING

- **Promotes a positive atmosphere:** Helps create and maintain a more positive environment, both at home and at work.

- **Encourages cooperation:** People are more likely to collaborate and actively participate when they feel motivated and positive about the situation.

- **Facilitates acceptance of changes:** Framing changes in a positive way can increase acceptance and reduce resistance.

- **Improves conflict resolution:** Approaching conflicts with a positive perspective can lead to more creative and less confrontational solutions.

Practice positive framing in your daily conversations. Try reframing a negative situation you recently discussed and notice how changing the presentation might alter the reaction of the people involved.

Ready to deepen your communication skills even further? In the next chapter, **"AVOIDING COMMUNICATION PITFALLS"** , we will explore how to identify and avoid patterns of language and behaviors that may be perceived as rude or disrespectful. This knowledge will be crucial to keeping your interactions as respectful as they are effective. Continue with us on this journey to become a more skilled and conscious communicator. Let's go!

AVOIDING COMMUNICATION PITFALLS

Communicating effectively requires not only knowing what to say and how to say it, but also being aware of the pitfalls that can sabotage your interactions. This chapter will address common language patterns and behaviors that may be perceived as rude or disrespectful, as well as offer strategies for avoiding them, ensuring that your communications are received in the most positive way possible.

KNOWING COMMON PITFALLS

- **Overgeneralizations:** Using words like "always" or "never" in discussions can lead to misunderstandings and defensive responses. These words suggest an absoluteness that is rarely accurate and can close the door to constructive dialogue.

- **Inappropriate tone of voice:** A tone of voice that sounds accusatory, sarcastic or condescending can turn a neutral conversation into a conflict. Attention to tone is crucial, especially in sensitive communications.

- **Frequent interruptions:** Interrupting others while they are speaking is not only seen as rude, but also as a sign that you do not value what they have to say.

- **Lack of positive feedback:** Communicating involves giving and receiving. Failing to recognize the contributions of others can leave them feeling unappreciated and reluctant to engage in future interactions.

- **Assumptions and presumptions:** Assuming you know what someone else is thinking or feeling without checking can lead to misunderstandings and resentment.

STRATEGIES TO AVOID THESE PITFALLS

- **Use specific language:** Avoid generalizations when discussing behaviors or situations. Be specific about what you are referring to, focusing on concrete instances rather than behaviors perceived as universal.

- **Control your tone:** Practice speaking calmly and clearly. Recording your own voice can help you become more aware of how you sound to others.

- **Practice active listening:** Show respect for others' points of view by listening carefully and waiting for them to finish speaking before responding.

- **Incorporate positive feedback:** Make a conscious effort to acknowledge and validate the contributions of others before offering your own perspective.

- **Check before assuming:** When you are unsure about someone's feelings or thoughts, ask directly instead of assuming. This shows respect for their experience and avoids misunderstandings.

Avoiding these pitfalls not only improves the quality of your interactions, but also strengthens your relationships by showing that you value and respect others. Integrating these practices into your daily life will require attention and effort, but the benefits for your communication will be immense.

Ready to continue improving your communication skills? In the next chapter, **"THE ART OF ASKING"** , we'll explore how to use questions effectively to guide conversations and clarify points that may seem obvious. This skill is essential for any effective communicator, helping to ensure that your interactions are as clear as they are constructive. Continue with us on this path of growth and development. Let's go!

THE ART OF ASKING

Asking questions is a powerful tool in communication. They not only help clarify doubts and deepen understanding, but also demonstrate interest and engagement. This chapter will focus on how you can effectively use questions to guide conversations, clarify points that may seem obvious, and significantly improve the quality of your interactions.

THE POWER OF QUESTIONS IN COMMUNICATION

Questions are essential for opening dialogues, exploring new ideas and resolving conflicts. They encourage reflection, stimulate the exchange of ideas and can alleviate situations in which direct information could be poorly received. Using questions effectively can completely transform the dynamics of a conversation.

TYPES OF QUESTIONS AND THEIR USES

- **Open-ended questions:** These questions generally begin with "how," "why," or "what" and are designed to encourage detailed responses. Example: "How do you think we can improve this process?"

- **Closed questions:** Used to obtain specific information, these questions can be answered with a simple "yes" or "no". Example: "Are you available for the meeting tomorrow?"

- **Reflective questions:** Used to reflect on what has been said, helping the person to explore their thoughts and feelings more deeply. Example: "You seem concerned about this decision; can you tell me more about your concerns?"

- **Clarifying questions:** They help to clarify what was said, ensuring that all participants in the conversation have the same understanding. Example: "When you say 'fast', can you specify a deadline?"

STRATEGIES FOR ASKING EFFECTIVE QUESTIONS

- **Be specific and direct:** Vague questions can lead to equally imprecise answers. Be clear and specific in what you are asking.

- **Use questions to build relationships:** Ask questions that show you value the opinions and experiences of others. This can strengthen relationships and increase trust.

Maintain a balance: While asking questions is essential, it is important not to turn the conversation into an interrogation. Let the conversation flow naturally.

- **Adjust the tone:** How you ask a question can affect how it is received. Make sure your tone is not interpreted as critical or condescending.

Implement what you learn by asking mindful questions in your everyday life. Practice in different contexts—with friends, family, or coworkers—and notice how questions can change the nature of a conversation.

Ready to continue developing your communication skills? In the next chapter, **"ASSERTIVENESS VS. AGGRESSIVENESS"**, we will explore the difference between being assertive and being aggressive. Learning to navigate between these two can help you express your needs and opinions respectfully and effectively. Continue with us on this journey to become an even more competent and conscious communicator. Let's go!

ASSERTIVENESS VS. AGGRESSIVENESS

Understanding the difference between being assertive and being aggressive is crucial to effective and respectful communication. Assertiveness involves expressing your ideas and needs clearly and directly, while respecting the rights and opinions of others. Aggressiveness, on the other hand, disregards the feelings of others and can lead to conflicts and misunderstandings. In this chapter, we will explore how you can cultivate assertive communication, avoiding aggression, to improve your interactions in all aspects of life.

UNDERSTANDING ASSERTIVENESS AND AGGRESSIVITY

- **Assertiveness** is the ability to express your thoughts and feelings in a confident and positive way, without being passive or aggressive. It's about being honest with yourself and others, always maintaining mutual respect.

- **Aggressiveness** , for its part, often involves imposing your opinions on others without considering their perspectives or feelings. This can result in defensive responses and can harm long-lasting relationships.

CHARACTERISTICS OF ASSERTIVE COMMUNICATION

- **Mutual respect:** Recognizes the importance of valuing both your own opinions and those of others.

- **Direct communication:** Clearly expresses your needs and desires bluntly, but respectfully.

- **Balance:** Maintains a healthy balance between expressing your feelings and considering those of others.

- **Openness to feedback:** You are open to receiving and discussing feedback in a constructive way.

CHARACTERISTICS OF AGGRESSIVE COMMUNICATION

- **Dominance:** Tries to control or dominate the conversation without considering other people's participation.

- **Intimidation:** Uses a raised tone of voice or language that may make others feel pressured or threatened.

- **Disregard:** Ignores or devalues the feelings and opinions of others.

- **Excessive defensiveness:** Responds to confrontations or criticism with hostility or anger.

TIPS FOR DEVELOPING ASSERTIVENESS

- **Know your rights and needs:** Be aware of your own needs and rights, as well as the rights of others.

- **Practice clear speech:** Use clear sentences that begin with "I feel", "I need" or "I would like", which express your needs without accusing or blaming others.

- **Stay calm and in control:** Even in tense situations, strive to remain calm and speak in a controlled manner.

- **Use positive feedback:** Include positive feedback in your interactions, which can help soften the impact of criticism or difficult requests.

Start small, choosing everyday situations where you can practice assertiveness. It could be something as simple as expressing a preference for a type of food or discussing a project at work. As you become more comfortable with being assertive in these smaller situations, you will find it easier to apply it in more challenging contexts.

Ready to advance your communication skills even further? In the next chapter, **"CONSTRUCTIVE FEEDBACK,"** we'll explore how to give and receive feedback in a way that's helpful and welcoming rather than critical and rude. Continuing to hone this skill is essential for any effective communicator. Let's keep learning together!

CONSTRUCTIVE FEEDBACK

Feedback is an essential tool for personal and professional growth. However, the way it is given and received can significantly influence its effectiveness and impact on relationships. This chapter explores techniques for offering and receiving feedback in a constructive and welcoming way, transforming potential moments of criticism into opportunities for development and learning.

UNDERSTANDING CONSTRUCTIVE FEEDBACK

Constructive feedback is feedback that aims to improve someone's performance or behavior by offering useful insights in a respectful and encouraging way. Unlike criticism, which often focuses on negative points and can be demotivating, constructive feedback is balanced, objective and focused on solutions.

ELEMENTS OF CONSTRUCTIVE FEEDBACK

- **Specific:** Avoid generalizations. Focus on specific examples to illustrate where and how the person can improve.

- **Balanced:** Include positive points along with areas for improvement to prevent the recipient from feeling undervalued.

- **Timely:** Offer feedback as close to the event in question as possible so details are still fresh and relevant.

- **Respectful:** Maintain a tone of respect and empathy. Remember, the goal is to help, not humiliate.

TIPS FOR PROVIDING FEEDBACK

- **Prepare:** Before offering feedback, think carefully about what you are going to say and how you are going to say it. This may include writing down key points to ensure clarity and brevity.

- **Contextualize:** Explain why you are offering feedback and how it can help the person achieve their goals or improve their performance.

- **Focus on the behavior, not the person:** Direct your comments to actions, not personal characteristics. For example, say "The report contained some errors that need to be corrected" instead of "You are not careful."

- **Promote a dialogue:** Encourage the person to express their vision and feelings about the feedback. This can increase mutual understanding and facilitate cooperation.

TIPS FOR RECEIVING FEEDBACK

- **Listen actively:** Even if it's difficult, try to listen carefully without interrupting or becoming defensive.

- **Ask for examples or clarifications:** If the feedback is unclear, ask for specific examples or a more detailed explanation.

- **Reflect:** Take time to think about the feedback you received. Honestly evaluate the points raised and consider how you can use them to grow.

- **Thank:** Regardless of whether you completely agree with the feedback or not, thank the person for bothering to share it.

Try applying these techniques in your daily life, both at work and in personal situations. Practice both the art of giving and receiving feedback. As you become more comfortable with these practices, you will find that they can lead to significant improvements in both your personal skills and interpersonal relationships.

Ready to move forward? In the next chapter, **"TRAINING PATIENCE AND CONTROL"**, we will explore how to develop patience and emotional control to deal with challenging communication situations. These skills are crucial for maintaining clear and respectful communication under pressure. Let's continue our path of learning and growth!

TRAINING PATIENCE AND CONTROL

Patience and emotional control are essential for effective communication, especially in challenging situations. Having the ability to remain calm and respond thoughtfully can prevent misunderstandings and reinforce positive relationships, both professionally and personally. This chapter offers guidance for developing these capabilities, allowing you to better manage your emotions and improve your interactions.

THE IMPORTANCE OF PATIENCE IN COMMUNICATION

Patience allows you to listen better, process information more completely, and respond more appropriately. This not only improves the quality of your responses, but also demonstrates respect and consideration for others' time and words, creating a more comfortable and conducive environment for dialogue.

STRATEGIES FOR DEVELOPING PATIENCE

- **Recognize triggers:** Identify which situations, behaviors or words tend to decrease your patience. Knowing these triggers can help you prepare calmer, more controlled responses.

- **Take a deep breath:** Simple breathing techniques can help calm the mind and reduce irritation. Practicing deep, slow breaths when you feel impatient can bring great relief.

- **Practice active listening:** Truly focusing on what is being said, rather than preparing your response while the other person is still speaking, can help develop patience and show genuine interest in the dialogue.

- **Establish intentional pauses:** Before responding in a conversation, consciously pause. This gives you time to think about the best way to respond and control immediate impulses.

THE IMPORTANCE OF EMOTIONAL CONTROL

Controlling your emotions means not allowing your responses to be guided by impulses or emotional states that can harm communication. This does not imply suppressing emotions, but understanding and managing your reactions in ways that are productive and respectful.

TECHNIQUES TO IMPROVE EMOTIONAL CONTROL

- **Self-knowledge:** Regularly reflect on your emotions and reactions. Try to understand why certain situations trigger strong emotional reactions in you.

- **Develop resilience:** Strengthen your ability to face emotional challenges by practicing resilience. This may include mindfulness techniques, meditation or therapy.

- **Assertive communication:** Use assertiveness to express your needs and emotions clearly and respectfully, without letting emotion dominate reason.

- **Ask for feedback:** Getting feedback on how your emotions affect your communication can offer valuable perspective and help you adjust your behavior.

Incorporate these strategies into your daily routine and in all your interactions. Over time, you will find that your ability to maintain patience and control your emotions will become stronger, leading to more effective communication and more harmonious relationships.

Ready to continue improving your communication skills? In the next chapter, **"MINDFULNESS TECHNIQUES IN COMMUNICATION"**, we will explore how mindfulness techniques can help you further improve clarity and kindness in speaking. Let's continue this journey of personal growth and communication skills together. Let's go!

MINDFULNESS TECHNIQUES IN COMMUNICATION

Mindfulness, or full attention, is the practice of being completely present and aware of the current moment, without judgment. By applying mindfulness techniques to communication, you can significantly improve the clarity of your messages and the way you respond to others, leading to more authentic and respectful interactions. This chapter explores how to incorporate mindfulness into your communicative practices to enhance both understanding and expression.

THE IMPORTANCE OF MINDFULNESS IN COMMUNICATION

Mindfulness helps you focus on the conversation, reducing distractions and improving your ability to listen and respond more effectively. Additionally, it allows you to recognize your own and others' emotions without reacting impulsively, facilitating more thoughtful and less reactive responses.

MINDFULNESS TECHNIQUES FOR EFFECTIVE COMMUNICATION

- **Full presence:** Make a conscious effort to be present during conversations. This means avoiding distractions, like checking your phone or thinking about other tasks while someone is talking.

- **Conscious listening:** Listen with the intention of understanding, not just responding. This involves paying attention not just to words, but also to tone of voice and body language, getting the full message.

- **Reflective response:** Before responding, pause briefly to consider what was said and how you feel about it. This pause can help you formulate a response that is truthful and respectful.

- **Self-observation:** Be aware of your own reactions during the conversation. Acknowledge any judgments or emotions that arise and try to understand how they may be influencing your perception and response.

- **Acceptance:** Accept the words and emotions of others without trying to change or judge them. This can help create an environment of trust and openness.

BENEFITS OF MINDFULNESS IN COMMUNICATION

- **Improved listening:** It makes you a more attentive and empathetic listener, which is essential for all relationships.

- **Reducing conflict:** By responding with mindfulness, you are less likely to overreact or defensively, which can reduce conflict.

- **Increased empathy:** Allows for greater connection with the feelings and perspectives of others, improving mutual understanding.

- **Clearer communication:** Helps you express your thoughts more clearly and directly, reducing the chances of misunderstandings.

Incorporate small mindfulness practices into your daily routine, such as mindful breaths before starting a conversation or moments of reflection after important interactions. Over time, these practices will become a natural habit, improving not only your communication but also your overall quality of life.

Ready to take another step forward? In the next chapter, **"PRACTICAL CASES: HOW TO SAY THE OBVIOUS WITHOUT BEING ROUGH"**, we will apply all the skills you learned to real-world examples. We'll explore specific work, family, and social media situations so you can see how these techniques are applied effectively. Stay with us to transform theory into practice and further improve your communication skills. Let's go!

PRACTICAL CASES: HOW TO SAY THE OBVIOUS WITHOUT BEING ROUGH

Effectively applying the communication techniques we've discussed so far is crucial, especially when it comes to expressing concepts or facts that may seem obvious. This chapter provides practical examples of how you can state the obvious without being rude, using common scenarios at work, family, and social media. Every situation is an opportunity to practice the art of communicating clearly and respectfully.

IN THE WORKPLACE

- **Situation:** Your colleague continues to send incomplete reports, something that has already been discussed previously.

- **Wrong approach:** "You always turn in incomplete reports. I don't know why I have to remind you of that."

- **Correct approach:** "I noticed that some points we discussed previously were left out of the last report. Let's review the criteria together to ensure we are on the same page? This could help improve our final delivery."

IN FAMILY RELATIONS

- **Situation:** A family member constantly forgets to do tasks that are important for organizing the house.

- **Wrong approach:** "You never remember to do what we ask. You don't seem to care about the order of the house."

- **Correct approach:** "I noticed that some tasks were pending again. I understand that we all have a lot on our minds. How about we put a reminder on our cell phone or a task board visible to everyone? That way, we can help each other remember."

ON THE SOCIAL NETWORKS

- **Situation:** Someone posts incorrect information that you know is a common misconception.

- **Wrong approach:** "This is completely wrong. How can you post something like this without checking?"

- **Correct approach:** "I understand the point you were making here and it's a really relevant topic! I saw additional information that could complement this topic and offer another perspective. Can I share it with you?"

GENERAL TIPS FOR SPEAKING THE OBVIOUS

- **Be empathetic:** Always try to understand why the other person doesn't understand what seems obvious to you. This can help formulate a more comprehensive approach.

- **Use questions:** Asking questions can help the other person reach a conclusion for themselves, which can be less confrontational than simply pointing out the error.

- **Offer help:** Instead of just pointing out what is wrong, offer solutions or help to improve the situation.

Maintain respect: Regardless of how obvious something may seem to you, maintaining respect for another's perspective is crucial.

By practicing these techniques in real situations, you will not only avoid being rude, but you will also build bridges of effective and respectful communication. In the next chapter, **"BUILDING BRIDGES, NOT WALLS"** , we will explore additional strategies for using communication as a tool to bring people together, even when there are disagreements. Stay with us on this journey to make every interaction more meaningful and respectful. Let's go!

BUILDING BRIDGES, NOT WALLS

Effective communication goes beyond simply conveying information; it has the power to unite people, transforming differences into points of connection and mutual understanding. This chapter focuses on strategies for using communication as a tool for unity, even in the face of disagreements and conflicts. By adopting these techniques, you can turn potential clashes into opportunities for collaboration and shared growth.

THE IMPORTANCE OF BUILDING BRIDGES

Building bridges through communication means creating bonds that promote understanding and cooperation rather than divisions. This is essential in all aspects of life, from personal interactions to global discussions, and requires a conscious and deliberate approach to overcome barriers and prejudices.

STRATEGIES FOR BUILDING BRIDGES

- **Focus on open dialogue:** Encourage the expression of different points of view in a respectful manner. Establish an environment where people feel safe to share their opinions without fear of judgement.

- **Practice active empathy:** Try to truly understand the other person's perspective, putting yourself in their shoes. This does not necessarily mean agreeing, but rather understanding the reasons behind your beliefs and behaviors.

- **Use of inclusive language:** Avoid words or phrases that may be exclusive or alienating. Choose language that includes all participants in the conversation, reinforcing the idea of a common goal.

- **Valuing differences:** Recognize and celebrate the differences between people as a source of strength and enrichment. Show how diverse points of view can contribute to more complete and innovative solutions.

- **Negotiation and compromise:** When faced with a conflict, seek solutions that meet the interests of all parties involved. This may involve compromises on both sides, but the result is often more lasting and satisfying.

APPLYING STRATEGIES IN PRACTICE

- **At work:** Use meetings to encourage the team to openly discuss project challenges, soliciting suggestions and emphasizing the importance of each contribution to the group's success.

- **At home:** When family disagreements arise, focus on understanding the emotions and perspectives involved. Use this to guide a conversation that seeks solutions acceptable to everyone.

- **In the community:** Participate in or organize discussion forums on local issues, where residents can express concerns and collaborate on action plans that benefit the community as a whole.

Building bridges through communication can lead to greater harmony and collaboration. Furthermore, by approaching conflicts and differences in a constructive way, you help create a more inclusive and welcoming environment, where everyone feels valued and heard.

Ready to move forward? In the next chapter, **"RESOLVING CONFLICTS WITH ELEGANCE"**, we will delve deeper into conflict resolution techniques, exploring how you can use communication to resolve disputes respectfully and effectively. Stay with us to further improve your communication skills and turn each challenge into an opportunity for growth. Let's go!

RESOLVING CONFLICTS WITH ELEGANCE

Conflicts are a natural part of human relationships, but the way they are resolved can strengthen or weaken bonds. The ability to resolve conflicts gracefully not only alleviates tensions but also fosters an environment of mutual understanding and cooperation. This chapter focuses on effective communication techniques that you can use to resolve disputes respectfully and efficiently.

UNDERSTANDING THE NATURE OF CONFLICTS

Conflicts arise when there are differences of opinions, values, or interests. They can be exacerbated by misunderstandings, ineffective communication or resource shortages. Recognizing the root of the conflict is the first step to resolving it effectively.

STRATEGIES FOR CONFLICT RESOLUTION

- **Active listening:** Listen to all parties involved without interruption. Often, just feeling heard can ease tension and pave the way for solutions.

- **Identification of common interests:** Focus on shared interests rather than defended positions. This can help find common ground where mutually beneficial solutions can be built.

- **Clear and assertive expression:** Communicate your thoughts and feelings clearly, using "I feel" or "I understand", avoiding accusations that could intensify the conflict.

- **Exploration of alternative solutions:** Encourage the generation of ideas where all parties contribute possible solutions. This not only increases the chance of finding an acceptable solution, but also promotes collaboration.

- **Formal agreement:** Once a solution is agreed, it is useful to formalize it through a written agreement or clear commitments. This ensures that everyone is aligned and committed to the proposed solution.

PRACTICAL EXAMPLES OF CONFLICT RESOLUTION

- **At work:** If two team members have conflicting ideas about the direction of a project, organize a meeting where each can present their visions and use a brainstorming approach to integrate elements of both ideas into a cooperative plan.

- **At home:** If there is a disagreement about household chores, discuss each person's preferences and establish a chore schedule that considers fairness and efficiency, allowing for adjustments as needed.

- **In the community:** In case of disputes about changes in the neighborhood, such as the implementation of new local policies, facilitate community meetings that provide space for everyone to express their concerns and suggestions.

Resolving conflicts gracefully strengthens relationships, promotes mutual respect, and creates a culture of open dialogue and constructive problem solving. This not only resolves the immediate conflict, but also improves the collective ability to deal with future discrepancies effectively.

Ready to advance on your journey of improving your communication skills? In the next chapter, **"CULTIVATING HUMILITY IN COMMUNICATION"** , we will explore the importance of humility when expressing opinions that seem obvious to you but may not be so clear to others. Stay with us and discover how humility can transform the way you interact and positively influence your communications. Let's go!

CULTIVATING HUMILITY IN COMMUNICATION

Humility is a powerful virtue in communication, especially when it comes to expressing opinions that may seem obvious to you but not to others. This chapter explores how to cultivate humility in your interactions, promoting a more respectful and effective exchange of ideas, and strengthening interpersonal relationships through recognizing and valuing others' perspectives.

THE IMPORTANCE OF HUMILITY IN COMMUNICATION

Humility in communication allows us to recognize that our own worldview is limited and that other people can offer valuable insights that escape us. Adopting a humble stance helps avoid unnecessary conflicts and facilitates more open and constructive dialogue.

CHARACTERISTICS OF A HUMBLE COMMUNICATOR

- **Attentive listener:** Shows genuine interest in other people's opinions, valuing everyone's contributions to the conversation.

- **Open to learning:** Recognizes that there is always something new to learn, regardless of experience or prior knowledge.

- **Ready to admit mistakes:** Accepts and admits mistakes without hesitation, seeing them as opportunities for personal and professional growth.

- **Avoid presumptions:** Avoid assuming that you know what is best for others or that your perspective is the only correct one.

PRACTICES TO DEVELOP HUMILITY IN COMMUNICATION

- **Ask more, assert less:** Encourage more dialogue and mutual discovery through questions that explore others' ideas and feelings, rather than just presenting your own opinions.

- **Value all contributions:** Make a conscious effort to recognize and value everyone's contributions, even if you don't agree with them. This not only promotes humility, but also encourages a more collaborative environment.

- **Reflect on your conversations:** After important conversations, take a moment to reflect on how you interacted. Ask yourself if you have been truly open and respectful of others' perspectives.

- **Practice self-awareness:** Stay aware of your own limitations and biases. Recognizing your own flaws is a crucial step in cultivating humility.

BENEFITS OF HUMILITY IN COMMUNICATION

- **Improves relationships:** Humility facilitates stronger and more respectful relationships, as people feel valued and understood.

- **Fosters mutual respect:** When people perceive your openness and respect for your ideas, they are more likely to reciprocate .

- **Encourages collaborative environments:** A humble approach to communication encourages an environment where collaboration and innovation can thrive.

- **Reduces conflicts:** By admitting that you don't have all the answers, you minimize the chances of conflicts based on misunderstandings or rigid opinions.

Ready to take your communication skills even further? In the next chapter, **"DEVELOPING GENTLE PERSUASION SKILLS"** , we will explore how you can positively influence others while maintaining a respectful and effective communication style. Continue with me on this journey of personal and professional enrichment. Let's go!

DEVELOPING GENTLE PERSUASION SKILLS

Persuasion is an essential art in communication, used to influence and convince others in a gentle and respectful way. This chapter is dedicated to teaching you how you can develop gentle persuasion skills, allowing you to present your ideas and convince others without imposing or aggressiveness.

THE NATURE OF GENTLE PERSUASION

Gentle persuasion differs significantly from more aggressive or manipulative approaches to influence. It is based on mutual respect, open dialogue and understanding the needs and desires of others, seeking to reach a consensus that benefits all parties involved.

STRATEGIES FOR EFFECTIVE AND RESPECTFUL PERSUASION

- **Know your audience:** Understanding who your interlocutors are and what they value is essential to adapt your message effectively.

- **Build credibility:** Show yourself trustworthy and well-informed. Credibility is essential to persuade, as people tend to trust and follow those who demonstrate knowledge and integrity.

- **Use logic and emotion:** Balance logical arguments with emotional appeals. People are influenced as much by data and facts as they are by stories and examples that resonate on an emotional level.

- **Be empathetic:** Demonstrate empathy and understanding for the perspectives and concerns of others. This can help break down resistance and build a bridge of understanding.

- **Practice active listening:** Listening attentively not only strengthens your arguments by responding directly to others' concerns , but also demonstrates respect and appreciation for others' opinions.

PRACTICAL EXAMPLES OF GENTLE PERSUASION

- **In the workplace:** When proposing a new initiative, present not only the benefits for the company, but also how it can meet the individual needs of colleagues or improve the work environment.

- **At home:** When discussing changes to your home routine, emphasize how these changes can provide more time for family activities or for each member to pursue their personal interests.

- **In the community:** When persuading neighbors to participate in a community project, highlight the collective and individual benefits, such as improved safety or local infrastructure.

BENEFITS OF GENTLE PERSUASION

- **Strengthened relationships:** Persuading in a gentle and respectful way strengthens relationships, as it creates an environment of cooperation and mutual respect.

- **Less resistance:** People are less defensive and more open to change when they feel respected and understood.

- **Greater influence:** By developing a reputation as a careful and considered communicator, your ability to influence within your social or professional circle grows significantly.

Ready for the next step? In the next chapter, **"DIGITAL COMMUNICATION AND ETIQUETTE"** , we will explore how to apply your communication skills in the digital age while maintaining courtesy and effectiveness on online platforms. Continue this journey of improvement to become an even more competent and influential communicator. Let's go!

DIGITAL COMMUNICATION AND ETIQUETTE

Digital communication has become a fundamental part of our lives, especially in today's interconnected world. In this chapter, we'll explore how you can apply your communication skills effectively across digital platforms while maintaining courtesy and clarity to ensure your online interactions are as respectful and productive as in-person interactions.

UNDERSTANDING DIGITAL COMMUNICATION

Digital communication includes emails, text messages, social media posts and interactions on video conferencing platforms. Each of these channels has its own norms and expectations, which can vary significantly depending on the context (professional or personal) and the audience.

BASIC PRINCIPLES OF DIGITAL LABEL

- **Clarity and conciseness:** Digital messages must be clear and direct. In professional settings, avoid overly casual language and jargon that could be misinterpreted.

- **Respect schedules:** Be aware of schedules when sending messages. Avoid sending professional communications outside of normal business hours unless it is an emergency.

- **Use of emojis and symbols:** In informal contexts, emojis can help convey the tone of the message, but in professional environments, their use should be limited and considered.

- **Proofread before sending:** Always re-read your messages before sending them to correct typographical, grammatical or tone errors.

- **Timely response:** Responding promptly to messages shows respect and consideration for the sender's time. Establish and maintain reasonable response time expectations.

ETIQUETTE IN PROFESSIONAL EMAILS

- **Clear subject:** The email subject field should be informative and specific to help the recipient understand the importance and context of the email.

- **Proper greeting:** Start with a formal greeting, unless you have a more casual prior relationship with the recipient.

- **Appropriate closing:** End your emails with a professional farewell, such as "Sincerely" or "Best regards", followed by your name.

ETIQUETTE ON SOCIAL MEDIA

- **Think before posting:** Reflect on the content of your posts and the impact they can have. Avoid posting something in an emotional impulse.

- **Privacy and security:** Consider privacy settings and who can see your posts. Respect the privacy of others by avoiding sharing information without permission.

- **Interact with respect:** Treat others with the same respect you would like to receive. Disrespectful or inflammatory comments are rarely productive.

BENEFITS OF GOOD DIGITAL LABEL

- **Improves understanding:** Clear and well-structured communication reduces misunderstandings.

- **Strengthens relationships:** Maintaining appropriate etiquette strengthens professional and personal relationships.

- **Promotes a positive image:** Good digital etiquette reflects positively on your personal and professional image.

Ready to explore more about effective communication? In the next chapter, **"OVERCOMING CULTURAL BARRIERS"**, we will discuss how cultural differences can affect the perception of what is obvious and how to navigate these situations. Join us to deepen your understanding and skills in a global context. Let's go!

OVERCOMING CULTURAL BARRIERS

Navigating communication between different cultures can be challenging, but it is essential for building effective and respectful relationships in a globalized world. This chapter explores how cultural differences can influence the perception of what is obvious and offers strategies for overcoming these barriers, ensuring more efficient and inclusive communication.

UNDERSTANDING CULTURAL BARRIERS

Cultural barriers in communication arise from differences in values, norms, and social expectations between different cultures. These differences can affect language, nonverbal expression, concepts of time and space, and even the way information is processed and understood.

IDENTIFYING COMMON CULTURAL DIFFERENCES

- **Direct vs. direct communication Indirect:** Some cultures value direct, clear communication, while others prefer more subtle, indirect approaches to avoid confrontation.

- **Individualism vs. collectivism:** Individualistic cultures tend to emphasize personal autonomy and individual responsibility, while collectivistic cultures focus on group well-being and community responsibilities.

- **High vs. low context low:** In high-context cultures, much communication is implicit and context-dependent, while in low-context cultures, communication is explicit and words directly express meaning.

- **Power relations:** Perceptions of hierarchy can vary significantly between cultures, influencing how communication is structured and who has authority to speak in different situations.

STRATEGIES TO OVERCOME CULTURAL BARRIERS

- **Education and knowledge:** Learn about the cultures you interact with regularly. Understanding customs, traditions and values can help you avoid misunderstandings and adapt your communication.

- **Flexibility and adaptation:** Be prepared to adjust your communication style as needed. This may mean being more direct or more subtle, depending on the cultural context.

- **Use of neutral language:** Avoid jargon, idiomatic expressions and cultural references that may not be understood by people from other cultures.

- **Clear feedback:** Encourage and practice getting feedback to ensure your message is understood as intended. This is especially important in intercultural interactions, where the chances of misunderstandings are greater.

- **Respect and sensitivity:** Show respect for cultural differences and be open to learning from others. Approaching cultural interactions with sensitivity and openness can transform challenges into opportunities for mutual enrichment.

BENEFITS OF OVERCOMING CULTURAL BARRIERS

- **Stronger relationships:** Effective communication across cultures strengthens personal and professional partnerships and relationships.

- **More inclusive environments:** When cultural barriers are overcome, a more welcoming and inclusive environment is created for everyone involved.

- **Opportunities for personal and professional growth:** The ability to communicate effectively across cultures is an increasingly valued skill in many professional fields.

Ready to move forward? In the next chapter, **"SELF-CARE AND SELF-AWARENESS"** , we will discuss how to maintain your mental and emotional health to ensure positive communication. Continue with us on this journey of continuous improvement of your intercultural communication skills. Let's go!

SELF-CARE AND SELF-AWARENESS

Maintaining good mental and emotional health is essential to communicating effectively. This chapter discusses the importance of self-care and self-awareness in communication, providing strategies to ensure you are always at your best, both for yourself and for others with whom you interact.

THE IMPORTANCE OF SELF-CARE IN COMMUNICATION

The emotional and mental state with which we enter a conversation can profoundly affect its course and outcome. Stress, fatigue, and emotional problems can impair our ability to listen actively, think clearly, and respond with empathy. Therefore, self-care is not only beneficial for ourselves, but also essential for maintaining healthy and productive interactions.

SELF-CARE STRATEGIES FOR COMMUNICATORS

> **- Stress management:** Regular stress management practices such as meditation, yoga, physical exercise or relaxing hobbies can help maintain calm and mental clarity.

> **- Adequate sleep:** A good night's sleep is crucial for cognitive and emotional functioning. Prioritize adequate rest to remain alert and attentive during interactions.

- **Healthy eating:** A balanced diet contributes to general well-being, which is directly linked to the ability to manage emotions and stress.

- **Healthy boundaries:** Learning to establish and maintain healthy boundaries is essential to avoiding burnout. This includes knowing how to say "no" and recognizing when you need a break.

- **Time for reflection:** Take time regularly to reflect on your interactions and feelings. This can help you identify communication patterns that you want to improve or change.

THE IMPORTANCE OF SELF-AWARENESS IN COMMUNICATION

Being self-aware means having a clear understanding of your own emotions, motivations, behaviors and the effect they have on others. In communication, self-awareness allows you to adjust your approach as needed, improve empathy, and respond more appropriately to the needs of the situation.

DEVELOPING SELF-AWARENESS

- **Regular feedback:** Request feedback from trusted people on how your communication is perceived. This can provide valuable insights that you may not be able to identify on your own.

- **Emotions and communication journal:** Keeping a record of your daily emotions and how they affect your communication can help you identify trends and triggers.

- **Mindfulness and meditation:** Mindfulness and meditation practices can significantly increase your awareness and control over your emotional and behavioral responses.

- **Training and workshops:** Attending training and workshops on communication and personal development can offer tools and techniques to increase self-awareness.

BENEFITS OF MAINTAINING SELF-CARE AND SELF-AWARENESS

- **Better quality of communication:** By taking care of yourself and understanding your own motivations, you improve your ability to communicate clearly and effectively.

- **Stronger relationships:** Improved communication leads to healthier, more fulfilling relationships.

- **Greater resilience:** Strengthening your emotional and mental well-being prepares you to better deal with communicative challenges.

Ready to advance further on your personal development and communication skills journey? In the next chapter, **"CREATING AN OPENING ENVIRONMENT"**, we will explore how to foster an environment where everyone feels comfortable expressing thoughts and ideas. Stay with us to learn how to create spaces for open and inclusive dialogue. Let's go!

CREATING AN OPENING ENVIRONMENT

Creating an environment where everyone feels comfortable expressing their ideas and opinions is essential for effective communication and the development of healthy and productive relationships, both personally and professionally. This chapter offers strategies for cultivating a space for open and inclusive dialogue, encouraging active participation and respectful sharing of perspectives.

THE IMPORTANCE OF AN OPEN ENVIRONMENT

An open communication environment promotes mutual trust and respect, crucial elements for the success of any team or personal relationship. When people feel safe expressing their ideas and concerns, there is a greater chance for innovation, effective problem solving, and interpersonal satisfaction.

STRATEGIES TO FOSTER OPENING

- **Establish communication norms:** Clearly define and communicate expectations and norms for communication within your group or team. This includes respect for all opinions, active listening and promoting constructive dialogue.

- **Promote active inclusion:** Make a conscious effort to include all voices in discussions, especially those who tend to be heard less. Encourage participation through direct questions and offer equal speaking time.

- **Create space for vulnerability:** Encourage an environment where sharing uncertainty, failures and fears is safe and seen as an important part of personal and professional growth.

- **Sensitivity and diversity training:** Implement regular training on diversity, inclusion and intercultural communication to raise awareness among team members about the importance of a welcoming environment.

- **Continuous and open feedback:** Cultivate a culture of open feedback where suggestions and concerns can be expressed freely and without fear of reprisal.

PRACTICAL EXAMPLES

- **At work:** During meetings, set aside a moment for a "check-in" where each team member can express how they feel or share something personal, helping to create human connections and openness.

- **At home:** Establish regular "family meetings" where everyone can discuss their days, concerns and achievements, ensuring that each family member has a voice.

- **In the community:** Organize community forums on relevant topics, where residents can express their opinions and ideas to improve the place where they live.

BENEFITS OF AN OPEN ENVIRONMENT

- **Improved collaboration and creativity:** An open environment encourages collaboration and creativity, as people feel free to explore new ideas.

- **Increased satisfaction and engagement:** When individuals feel that their voices are heard and valued, there is a natural increase in satisfaction and engagement.

- **More effective conflict resolution:** An open dialogue space makes conflict resolution easier as issues are discussed openly before they escalate.

Ready to continue developing an effective communicative environment? In the next chapter, **"RECEIVE AND INTEGRATE FEEDBACK"** , we'll explore how to accept and use feedback to continually improve your interactions. Follow us to learn more about how to turn feedback into constructive action. Let's go!

RECEIVE AND INTEGRATE FEEDBACK

Feedback is a vital tool for personal and professional growth, providing valuable insights into how your actions and communications are perceived by others. This chapter explores how you can effectively receive and integrate feedback, turning it into constructive action to improve your communication and interaction skills.

THE IMPORTANCE OF RECEIVING FEEDBACK

Accepting feedback — especially when it's critical — can be challenging, but it's essential for continued development. It offers an outside perspective that can highlight blind spots in our behavior and communication, allowing for adjustments that improve our relationships and effectiveness.

STRATEGIES FOR RECEIVING FEEDBACK IN A CONSTRUCTIVE WAY

- **Keep an open mind:** Approach feedback with an attitude of learning, not defense. View it as an opportunity to grow, not a personal criticism.

- **Actively listen:** Listen without interrupting. Even if you disagree with some points, allow the person giving the feedback to fully express their observations.

- **Ask for clarification:** If something is not clear, ask for specific examples or more details. This can help you better understand feedback and identify specific areas for improvement.

- **Thank them for the feedback:** Regardless of whether you agree with the feedback or not, thank the person for sharing it. Recognizing someone's effort to help you is essential to maintaining positive relationships.

- **Create an action plan:** After receiving the feedback, reflect on how you can apply it in practice. Set specific, measurable goals to implement the suggested changes.

INTEGRATING FEEDBACK INTO YOUR DEVELOPMENT

- **Set improvement goals:** Based on the feedback you receive, set clear and achievable goals to improve your specific skills or behaviors.

- **Seek additional resources:** If feedback indicates areas that require significant improvement, consider seeking courses, books, or even a mentor to help you develop these skills.

- **Monitor your progress:** Establish regular checkpoints to assess your progress against established goals. Adjust your strategies as needed.

- **Request ongoing feedback:** Development is an ongoing process. Keep asking for feedback regularly to ensure you're on the right track and to adjust your action plan as you evolve.

BENEFITS OF INTEGRATING FEEDBACK

- **Continuous improvement:** Integrating feedback effectively ensures you are always learning and improving.

- **Reinforced relationships:** By demonstrating that you value and act on feedback, you strengthen trust and respect in your relationships.

- **Improved performance:** By adjusting your behavior and communication techniques, you improve your overall performance, both personally and professionally.

Ready for the next step? In the next chapter, **"CONCLUSION AND THE WAY FORWARD"** , we will summarize the key points covered in this book and discuss how you can continue to practice and improve your clear and respectful communication skills. Stay with us to consolidate your learning and prepare for future success. Let's go!

CONCLUSION AND THE WAY FORWARD

Congratulations on getting this far! Throughout this book, we explore a wide range of techniques and strategies for improving communication, with a special focus on how to state the obvious clearly and respectfully without being rude. In this final chapter, we'll summarize the key points and discuss how you can continue to improve your communication skills in your everyday life.

REVIEW OF KEY POINTS

- **Effective communication:** We learned the importance of being clear and direct, while being empathetic and respectful towards our interlocutors.

- **Active listening and empathy:** We highlight how active listening and empathy are crucial to truly understanding and appropriately responding to the needs of others.

- **Assertiveness vs. aggressiveness:** We explore the difference between being assertive and being aggressive, emphasizing the importance of expressing our own needs and opinions in a positive way.

- **Constructive feedback:** We've seen how offering and receiving feedback in a constructive way can be a powerful tool for personal and professional growth.

- **Cultural adaptation:** We discuss how to overcome cultural barriers to improve communication in diverse contexts.

CONTINUING DEVELOPMENT

The path to becoming an effective communicator is ongoing and requires constant practice. Here are some tips to maintain your growth:

- **Regular practice:** Apply the techniques learned regularly, both in personal and professional contexts. The more you practice, the more natural it will become.

- **Seeking feedback:** Keep asking for feedback on your communication skills. Use it to adjust and improve your behavior.

- **Continuing education:** Attend workshops, courses, and additional reading to deepen your communication knowledge and skills.

- **Personal reflection:** Take time regularly to reflect on your interactions. Ask yourself what worked, what didn't, and what you can do differently next time.

- **Mentoring:** Consider finding a mentor or communications coach who can guide you through your personal and professional development.

Every step you take to improve your communication opens new doors to success and satisfaction in all areas of your life. I encourage you to remain committed to using communication not just to express ideas, but to build bridges of mutual understanding and respect. Continue the learning journey, always keeping an open mind, a heart willing to understand, and the desire to improve.

Thank you for taking the time to learn and grow from this book. I hope the skills gained here accompany you on all your communication journeys, making every conversation an opportunity to develop deeper, more meaningful connections. Good luck, and continue communicating with clarity, courage and care. Let's move on!

As we turn the final page of this journey together, I sincerely hope that the learnings shared here have touched your heart and sparked new perspectives. If this book has brought you any value, I kindly ask that you take a few moments to leave a review on Amazon. Your words not only help me grow and hone my craft, but they also guide other readers in their quests for knowledge and inspiration. Your opinion is a valuable gift, both for me and for the community of readers looking for stories that transform. I sincerely thank you for sharing this journey with me and I hope we can meet again in the pages of a new adventure.

REGINALDO OSNILDO

Hello, I'm Reginaldo Osnildo, author and innovator in the areas of sales, technology, and communication strategies. My experience ranges from the academic environment, as a professor and researcher at the University of Southern Santa Catarina, to practice as a strategist at Grupo Catarinense de Rádios. With a PhD in sales narratives and digital convergence, and a master's degree in storytelling and social imaginary, I bring my readers a unique fusion of theory and practice. My goal is to provide knowledge in a simple, practical and didactic language, encouraging direct application in personal and professional life.

Yours sincerely

Reginaldo Osnildo

www.ingramcontent.com/pod-product-compliance
Lightning Source LLC
Chambersburg PA
CBHW071100240526
45471CB00016B/2214